THE ESSENTIAL BOOK OF

MOON MAGIC

THE ESSENTIAL BOOK OF

MOON MAGIC

Harness the gift of lunar energy

MARIE BRUCE

SIRIUS

SIRIUS

This edition published in 2024 by Sirius Publishing, a division of
Arcturus Publishing Limited,
26/27 Bickels Yard, 151–153 Bermondsey Street,
London SE1 3HA

ISBN: 978-1-3988-3670-9
AD011088UK

Printed in China

Contents

Introduction

Per Ardua Ad Astra
(Through Adversity to the Stars)

Welcome to the world of moon magic, where the night sky shines bright with possibility and shooting stars herald the arrival of new opportunities. Witches have always worked with the power of the moon. We use its pull to manifest our goals and to draw positive things into our lives. Working with lunar energy is an intrinsic part of spell casting and pagan rituals.

The night sky is full of mystery and magic, beauty and magnificence. To be spellbound, all you have to do is look up and gaze at the stars or the orb of the full moon. *Per ardua ad astra* is a Latin phrase which loosely translates to mean *through adversity to the stars*, and while this phrase is perhaps best known for being the motto of the Royal Air Force, it can also be a good mantra for anyone who wishes to improve their life using the magic of the moon and stars.

Life can be difficult at times and everyone is going through something, but with magic at your fingertips you can take steps to minimize the negative events and maximize the positive outcomes in your life. In this book you will learn how to set up a magical moon altar, how to tap into

the power of the lunar cycle and how to use moon magic to manifest your goals. In addition, you will find meditations, rituals, totem animals and dream-weaving spells, allowing you to make the very most of the night sky and the power of the moon goddess, each and every night of your life. It's time to embrace the moon-cast shadows and tap into your nocturnal power, with the enchanting practice of Moon Magic.

This is a world where sweet dreams come true!

Serene Blessings
Marie Bruce x

CHAPTER ONE
WITCH'S MOON

I s there anything more beautiful than the sight of a full moon on a clear night? The moon is the most recognizable part of our universe and one that even the smallest child can identify. Other planets may remain a mystery, but the moon is our close companion. She watches over us as we sleep, she lights the sky at night, beaming her silvery glow over the world, creating an enchanted landscape. She provides vital illumination for soldiers on night missions and casts a romantic glow over lovers in the gloaming, sharing their first kiss. She is a gentle, yet powerful presence, pulling at the tides with her magnetic force, waxing and waning as she moves in orbit around the earth.

The moon and magic go hand in hand. Images of witches dancing naked under the full moon were often used as propaganda during the witch hunts of the past, and even today, we are bombarded with pictures of witches flying across the moon on broomsticks every October in the run-up to Halloween. While broomstick flight might be no more than a flight of fancy, there is some truth in the naked dancing, for covens of witches sometimes like to work naked, or skyclad as it is also known, when celebrating seasonal changes. This lack of clothing denotes the freedom of birth and the natural state, but it is by no means compulsory. You can perform moon magic just as effectively while remaining fully dressed, and on a dark winter's night; warm clothing is certainly advised!

WITCHES AND THE MOON

Witches have a very special relationship with the moon. While we do not *worship* her as such, we do cast our spells in accordance with the lunar

cycle, each phase being used for a particular type of magic. We hold special rituals, called Esbats, to mark the new and full lunar phases each month. We see the moon as being representative of the divine feminine, hence why we refer to her with feminine pronouns. She is known as the Lady or the Goddess and she is a vital force of magic that witches tap into when casting spells or performing rituals.

Rarely does a witch cast a spell without first consulting a lunar calendar to see where the moon is in her cycle. We cast magic in her light, drawing on her power to magnetize the things we dream of and bring them into being. If the earth is our mother, then the moon is our grandmother. We connect with her through the constant changes of the lunar cycle, pulling things towards us as she waxes to full, then releasing the things that no longer serve us as she wanes to dark moon. In this way, we are always connected to her lunar energies.

CREATE A LUNAR ALTAR

Setting up a lunar altar in your home is a great way to connect with the moon's power. Having a special place dedicated to the moon and your magical practice is one of the ways you can begin to invite the magical light of the moon into your life.

Begin by collecting items which depict or represent the moon, so postcards, pictures, ornaments, candle holders, crystals, mirrors and so on. Find a place in your home to use as a moon altar. This could be a windowsill, a countertop or a small side table. You might like to cover it with a white or silver cloth, but this is optional. Next, arrange all your

items in a pleasing way, ensuring that you have a couple of candles ready to burn, placed towards the back of the altar. Add an incense burner and your altar is ready for magical use.

You can use this space to cast spells, perform rituals, lay out divination card spreads and light incense in honour of any lunar deities you are working with. Add a statue of the lunar totem animals you connect with too, and make this a space that is personal to you and your magical moon journey. Finally, bless the space by sprinkling a little spring water over the altar and saying the following words:

> *'I dedicate this sacred space to the*
> *lunar light of the moon's magical grace'*

THE LUNAR CYCLE

In order to cast with the power of the moon, you first need to understand her cycle and how she works. The moon takes around 27 days to complete one full orbit around the earth. It also takes approximately 29 days to go from one new moon to the next – this is called a lunar month. Already, you can see the parallels between the lunar cycle and the female menstrual cycle. This is another one of the reasons why the moon is referred to in the feminine. Magically speaking, each point in the lunar cycle represents an aspect of spell-casting, which are as follows:

New Moon

This is the beginning of the lunar cycle, although the moon cannot actually be seen in the sky until a few days after the new moon. For this reason, the start of the new moon phase is sometimes known as dark moon and is typically a time of rest. As soon as the first sliver of light appears, however, it is time to start thinking about what you want the next lunar cycle to bring you. The new moon is a time for sowing the seeds of new projects, weighing up the pros and cons of a situation, assessing the need for a change in your patterns etc. Remember that all seeds are sown in darkness, to grow with the light. Now is the time to decide what you want.

Waxing Crescent

The light increases from the right, showing a crescent moon that looks like a backwards C shape. This is the time when you set your intention – set your mind on exactly what it is you want. You don't need to know how you will achieve the goal, just set your intention and allow the universe to work out the details for you.

First Quarter Moon

In this phase the moon looks like it has been cut in half – half of it is illuminated by the sun, the other half remains in darkness. Now is the time to take action on your intentions, so brush up your CV or start applying for jobs if a career change is your goal. Make a positive start on a new project. Get out more and meet new people if you want to draw friends to you. Make a start on your goal, even if only in a small way.

Waxing Gibbous

The moon now appears to be three quarters full, with most of it brightening our night sky. Now is the time to start walking your talk. It's not enough to have a goal; you need to take consistent action and work towards it. The lunar energies won't do the work for you! It is a collaboration, and you need to put the effort in too. At this time, the energies are growing stronger and magnetically pulling in your intention, so help it along with positive action.

Full Moon

The full moon lights up the night sky, and her effect can be felt by everyone, all over the world. This is a time of abundance, of goals coming to fruition and labouring on long-term ambitions. The full moon offers a boost of energy if you are flagging on your aspirations, lending much-needed energy to your goal. The energy of the full moon can be felt for three nights in a row – the night before, the night of, and the night after the moon is full. This is also the most powerful time for all kinds of magic, divination and spell casting, so don't waste it!

Waning Gibbous

As the moon begins to wane, now is the time to show gratitude for what this lunar cycle has brought you so far. Reflect on what worked and what projects are still in progress. Big ambitions take more than one lunar cycle to manifest, so use this time to assess where you are on the path to achievement and reflect on what your next steps should be. Think about what has worked well for you and what you would like to change or do better at in the next lunar cycle.

Last/Third Quarter Moon

This is the time to start releasing anything that no longer serves you. Let go of old grudges, bad relationships, mistakes made, toxic habits and so on. In this phase, the moon requires you to be honest with yourself, to identify the toxic behaviours and bad habits that might be contributing to a negative situation, so that you can release those too.

Waning Crescent/Balsamic Moon

This phase marks the end of the lunar cycle, when the moon shows up in the sky as the classic fairy-tale C-shaped crescent. It is a time to reflect and move deeper into self-awareness. This is a good time to cast banishing spells as the moon's energy helps to pull things away from you. Slowly the light will fade out, night by night, until we are back at the dark moon and the cycle begins once more, so it is never too late for a fresh start and each moon cycle offers a new opportunity to begin again.

As you learn more about the phases of the moon you will come to understand how it affects you personally. You might find that you are full of beans and ideas shortly after the new moon, but your enthusiasm wanes after the full moon. Many people report experiencing vivid dreams during the full moon. Keep a note of any special experiences you have and where the moon was in her cycle at the time. Be aware that the moon is in the same phase all over the world. Remember that the moon's energies can still be felt by day too. She is always there, influencing us from above, even though we can't always see her bright orb in the sky. Her power is constant, though her appearance is ever changing.

CHAPTER TWO
MOON LORE

T hroughout the centuries the moon has held a captive audience here on earth, as people gaze up and try to interpret her movements, attributing it with personal significance. In the years since the moon landing in 1969, we have come to understand her from a more scientific perspective, but for our ancestors, she was an icon of mystery and magic. Over the years, many superstitions evolved, from paying tribute to the moon to ward away bad luck, to using her cycle as a way of keeping time, in the days before the calendar was invented. In this chapter we will look at some of the popular folklore that has been influenced by the mystery of the moon.

NAME THAT MOON

Long before the calendar we know today was invented, people used the moon as a way of keeping track of time and marking the passing seasons. They did this by giving each full moon a special name. In this way they tracked the cycle of the seasons, each month having a moon which was named for the seasonal changes of that time of the year. Even the word *month* is derived from the word moon, so each year was divided into moons or months. Some of these lunar names are still in use today. We might talk of the harvest moon or the wolf moon, for instance. Although there are slight variations in the names for each moon from region to region, two naming systems have stood the test of time: the traditional country names and the shamanic names of Native Americans. In naming each full moon, it became a reflection of what was happening on the earth during that time, as you will see from the following examples:

TRADITIONAL COUNTRY MOONS

January – Wolf Moon

February – Storm or Ice Moon

March – Chaste, Worm or Death Moon

April – Seed or Growing Moon

May – Hare or Flower Moon

June – Dryad or Strawberry Moon

July – Mead or Buck Moon

August – Wyrt or Barley Moon

September – Harvest Moon or Corn Moon

October – Hunter's or Blood Moon

November – Snow or Beaver Moon

December – Oak, Cold or Winter's Moon

SHAMANIC MOONS

Although the actual dates vary for the shamanic moons, usually beginning on the 10th or 11th of the month, they can roughly be divided like so:

January – Deep Snows Moon

February – Strong Winds Moon

March – Fast Water-flow Moon

April – Planting Moon

May – Flowering Moon

June – Drying Up Moon

July – Hot Winds Moon

August – Hunter's Moon

September – Ripening Moon

October – Harvest Moon

November – Popping Trees Moon

December – Hard Freeze Moon

As you can see, the same seasonal themes occur within both traditions, so there are moons for harvest, hunters, snow, ice and the new growth of spring. In this way the moon acted as a vital prompt, reminding people when to plant, when to bring in the crops, when to slaughter livestock or hunt for meat and when to retreat indoors as the winter weather closed in.

The moon was a visual cue for the agricultural year and the tasks required to ensure survival. Only a fool would leave livestock in the fields during the Wolf Moon, when the wolves of old would come closer to villages in search of food. Instead, animals would be brought into barns and shelters closer to the homestead, where they could be watched over more easily, safe from the hungry pack. While we no longer have to worry about wolves roaming through our gardens and snacking on the pet rabbit, it is still beneficial to learn these old names for the full moon of each month because it reinforces our link with the land and connects us to our ancestors. This is the lunar calendar which they would have lived by.

ATTUNING WITH THE MOON

Try to spend a little time each evening attuning with the energies of the moon. Go outside and bathe in her light. Breathe it in. Learn to recognize what phase she is in simply by looking at the night sky. This might take some time, but practice makes perfect! Feel how the energy changes as the moon goes through the various stages of her cycle. Once you have been doing this for several months, begin to test yourself by trying to guess the lunar phase when you are indoors, without looking through the window or using your phone! Can you pick up on the lunar energies? Can you *feel* what phase the moon is in?

Attuning with the moon in this way can help to sharpen your instincts and hone your skills of perception. Bear in mind that we are instinctively drawn to her power, and spending time beneath the moonlight is as natural as sunbathing on a hot day. Try not to get spooked by the wildlife, who are more active during the darker hours, and make sure that you are in a safe space, such as your garden.

LUNAR SUPERSTITIONS

A superstition is the common belief that something has a supernatural power to bring about either good or bad luck. In the past, the world was a naturally much more superstitious place, because we didn't have a lot of science to make sense of our environment. Failed crops, plagues, pandemics and destructive weather patterns were often regarded as signs of witchcraft or demonic interference.

To counteract these ill favours, people came up with common practices that were thought to keep such bad luck at bay. These practices might involve carrying a charm to attract good luck or ward away evil, or never stepping into the shadow of a suspected witch, for instance.

Fear of the unknown, ignorance, and events which couldn't be explained in a pre-scientific era led people to develop their own forms of comfort, and the common superstition was born. Many of these super-stitious practices became so well known that some people still adhere to them today, without even thinking about it. For example, when was the last time you walked under a ladder? You probably didn't. You probably walked around it, because superstition states that to walk beneath a ladder is bad luck!

Unsurprisingly, the moon has attracted quite a few superstitions of her own, ranging from the belief that the full moon causes madness to the more benevolent trope that lovers who first kiss beneath a full moon are blessed. Let's take a look at a few more lunar superstitions:

☽ It is unlucky to see a new moon through a window. If this happens you should open the window and invite the lunar light into your home as an honoured guest.

☽ The time of the full moon is said to bring about prophetic dreams, especially if you sleep in the moon's rays, while the dreams you have during the waning or dark moon tend to highlight your fears and concerns and are more likely to turn into nightmares.

☽ It is said to be unlucky to point directly at the moon, but blowing her a kiss will bring good fortune your way.

☽ Seeing the full moon swathed in mist is a sign of trouble to come, which can be alleviated by saying, '*Mother Moon in the mist, blink clear your eye and send no sorrow to my loved ones and I.*'

☽ Seeing a halo around a full moon indicates a sharp frost and a colder turn in the weather.

☽ The full moon of March is sometimes known as the Death Moon because it represents the end of winter.

☽ Spotting the moon over your shoulder is bad luck. You should turn around and face the moon directly, giving her a nod, to turn the bad luck away.

☽ A full moon on a Monday is extremely auspicious and heralds a month of good fortune, while a full moon on a Sunday heralds the opposite.

》 It is unlucky for a woman to travel across water on a full moon unless she is a witch, as bad luck will surely follow her. This is an old sailors' superstition and is akin to it being bad luck to have a woman on board a ship at all!

》 To see the black disk of a dark moon means that a storm is coming.

》 Turning your coins over in the light of a new moon brings prosperity for the rest of the month.

》 Never pay your bills during a waning moon or the money will not return to you. Pay them during a waxing moon and the cash will return threefold.

》 Always cut your hair during a waxing moon to ensure it grows back thick and healthy.

》 Brushing your hair in moonlight is said to enhance your allure.

》 Seeing the moon reflected in a body of water such as a lake, loch or the sea is a sign of emotional upheaval to come.

》 To see a red moon is a sign of bad luck.

BOWING TO THE MOON

In many magical traditions and esoteric practises, it is customary to make some kind of abeyance to the moon. From the lunar salutations of yoga to the Wiccan practice of an Esbat ritual, acknowledging the moon in some way is thought to be a beneficial practice and it is also said to bring about good fortune. Typically, an abeyance would be made at both the new and full moon, but you can acknowledge her light every night if you wish. Bowing to the moon is a traditional practice in some Eastern religions, while in the West it was more common to give a nod. Whatever way you decide to make your abeyance, the important thing is that you acknowledge the moon in some way, particularly when she is new and also at her fullest; so just pretend you've dropped something and bow down in her light – no-one else need ever know that you have just offered a salutation to the moon!

MOON MADNESS

The notion that the moon can contribute to crazy behaviour has been in play for a long time. Perhaps it is no more than an urban myth, but many professional people, be they vets, midwives or police officers, claim that a full moon marks a much busier time.

It is commonly believed that a full moon has such a powerful influence on human behaviour that there are more accidents, crimes and random acts of violence committed, more births and emergencies etc. during the time of the full moon, but this idea has never been scientifically proven. It could simply be that the bright light of a full moon

leads to more people being out and about much later into the evening, resulting in a corresponding spike in incidents, but it certainly makes you wonder doesn't it?

For centuries the moon has been thought to cause madness, hence the word *lunatic*, which of course derives from the word *lunar*, from which we get the modern terminology of lunacy, loony or loon, all used to denote someone of questionable sanity. Then of course there is the werewolf legend, where people turn into crazy monsters around the time of the full moon!

It can be difficult to separate fact from fiction when it comes to the moon's influence on human behaviour, but it would be crazy not to even consider it as a possibility. The moon has an effect on the ocean tides, and many people garden and plant crops at certain points of the lunar phase to make the most of these magnetic lunar energies, so why wouldn't the moon have an effect on us too? Much more research needs to be done before we can say one way or the other, but until it is a categorically disproven theory, people all over the world will still believe that the full moon makes some individuals behave in very odd ways!

As you can see from this chapter, the moon has held our imagination captive for hundreds of years, and we have a wealth of superstition and folklore as a result of our fascination with this bright lunar orb. Despite all that we know of her scientifically, she has still maintained an air of mystery and magic, drawing us into her light with promises of enchantment and luck. Just don't forget to bow in abeyance every now and then!

CHAPTER THREE
LUNAR DEITIES

Since ancient times many of the planets and celestial bodies have been attributed to gods and goddesses. These deities are the personification of those planetary energies. They were invoked by practitioners who wanted to connect with those energies or request a special boon from the deity. The moon is no different, and there are lots of deities associated with it. Because the moon is regarded as a feminine energy, most lunar deities are goddesses, but there are a few lunar gods too, as you will see in this chapter.

TRIPLE GODDESS

For pagans and witches, the moon represents the Triple Goddess, or Three in One. The Triple Goddess is made up of the Maiden, the Mother and the Crone. The lunar cycle can be split between these three aspects of the goddess. From new to just before full moon is the time of the Maiden; full moon is the time of the Mother; waning to dark moon is the time of the Crone. Each aspect of the Triple Goddess represents different energies and can be invoked for different purposes.

The Maiden

The Maiden is the goddess of youthfulness, innocence and fresh starts. She can help you get in touch with your inner child or adopt a more optimistic and youthful approach to life. She is the ingénue, for whom

the world is a new discovery. She encourages us to try new things, take up new hobbies and experiences, and step bravely into new environments and situations. She is a breath of fresh air, the dawning of sexuality, fertility and romance. Her light is a silver crescent in the night sky; her pull is the incoming tide.

You might feel her energies as a certain restlessness, or itchy feet, during the new to waxing moon. Act on this restlessness and use her energies to try something new. Explore and go adventuring, book a holiday to a place you've never been before or take up a new hobby. All things new and uncharted come under the domain of the Maiden, so embrace it with a sense of exploration.

The Mother

The Mother represents the fruition of fertility, abundance, wealth, plenty, growth and expansion. She is the natural abundance of the harvest, the fruit of the orchard and the swelling seas of high tide. As the moon is round and full during the time of the Mother, it represents the growth of pregnancy, the anticipation of parenthood and the expectation of abundance in all things.

The Mother is all nurturing, encouraging you to perform acts of kindness to others and to practice self-care skills. New projects now begin to show considerable promise and you might begin to enjoy the fruits of past labours during the time of the Mother phase. Her energies can be felt as a deep sense of contentment and faith that all will be well. She brings unexpected blessings, especially those that increase comfort and abundance, so look out for sudden windfalls and lovely invitations, as the Mother provides for you. Allow her to guide you towards a sense of peace and plenty.

The Crone

The Crone is the goddess of endings and darkness, of ebb tide and midnight. As the moon wanes to dark, its light shrinks to nothing, leaving the skies black as black for a short time. The Crone is perhaps the most misunderstood aspect of the Triple Goddess – she certainly seems to be the most feared by non-magical people! But their fears are unfounded, for the Crone is simply darkness and rest. She is the force that takes away all that no longer serves you and, like the wind that strips the dead wood from trees, she is necessary to make room for new growth. She encourages you to let go and move on. She is the wisdom of the elder, the prophecy of the seer, the magic of the sorceress. She is powerful and strong, despite her aged appearance.

You might feel her energies as a sudden desire to declutter your home, or in a sharp lesson learnt. The Crone does not suffer fools gladly, and her power will bring the life-lessons needed to make you stronger and more resilient, for she is a galvanizing force to be reckoned with. She is not without compassion, though, and she encourages you to take the rest that you need, when you need it, so you might sleep more during a waning or dark moon, or feel a sense of lethargy.

As a goddess of the Underworld, she is associated with death, and so you might feel the need to make a will, take out life insurance or get your

finances in order during her phase, not because death is imminent, but because she asks us to face the unknown with courage and prepare for the unexpected. The energies of the Crone are good for banishing things from your life – bad habits, old patterns of behaviour, toxic friends etc. She expects you to make space for the blessings that are to come, so that you are ready to receive the fruit of the seeds that are sown during her darkness.

ARTEMIS

The Greek Artemis is one of the most well-known moon goddesses. She is associated with the hunt, carrying a bow and arrows and linked to deer, hares and hounds, which are all her totem animals. The crescent moon is regarded as her bow in the night sky. Artemis is a virgin goddess who maintained her chastity. She is seen as a self-sufficient deity of great independence, and one who finds her own path. The Greek Priestesses of the Moon were also expected to remain virgins, and Artemis was extremely vengeful if any of them were abused, or fell from grace in any way. Artemis was said to have helped her mother give birth to her twin brother Apollo, whilst she was only a baby herself, so she is also associated with childbirth too, despite being a virgin goddess. She can be invoked for spells of independence, chastity and childbirth.

ARIANRHOD – SILVER WHEEL

Arianrhod is a Welsh goddess associated with the moon and sometimes known as the Lady of the Silver Wheel. This Wheel is thought to represent the turning of time and the weaving of fate and destiny. Arianrhod's silver oar wheel was also the means by which the dead were carried into the afterlife and she is known as a goddess of reincarnation. She is linked with the North Star and therefore with guidance during times of trauma. Like many Celtic goddesses, Arianrhod was skilled in needlecraft, particularly weaving, and she is the weaver of the cosmic web. Mythology tells us that she lived in a castle in the polar region of stars, known as Caer Sidi, and that she rode a snowy-white chariot through the heavens to watch over the tides that she governed. Her feast day falls on 2nd December each year, and so she is also a goddess of winter. The appearance of the Aurora Borealis is a sign that she is near, and her totem animal is a pure-white owl. Although not one of the virgin goddesses, Arianrhod was an independent deity who would not share her power with a consort. She can be called upon for guidance, autonomy and winter moon magic.

SELENE

Selene was one of the original Greek Titan goddesses, which were the most powerful deities of all and regarded as being the creators of the universe. Selene was a moon goddess, and she held dominion over the night sky and the heavens. In the Roman pantheon her counterpart's name is simply Luna. In Wicca she is often worshipped during the Esbat rituals of new and full moons. In mythology, Selene is said to drive her

silver chariot, pulled by white horses or unicorns, across the sky each night, casting out dreams and blessings as she goes. Selene fell in love with Endymion, a young shepherd boy. She cast a sleeping spell upon him so that she might visit him in secret each night, without revealing herself to a mortal man. Because of this, Selene is also regarded as a goddess of romance and of difficult or secret love affairs. Invoke her for sweet dreams, new romance, manifestation and general good blessings.

SIN

Sin, also known as Suen, Nanna or Nannar, is the Mesopotamian god of the moon. He was revered in ancient times throughout Eastern civilizations, including Babylon and Arabia. His totem animal was the bull, and all cattle fell under his protection, as did the herdsmen who watched over the herd. Sin was the father of the better-known goddess, Inanna or Ishtar, who was known as the Queen of Heaven. She is a significant figure in Wicca.

MANI

Interestingly, in Norse mythology the deities for sun and moon are subverted, with Mani being the god of the moon and his sister, Sol, being the goddess of the sun. Both Mani and Sol were fathered by a mortal man who was so taken by their good looks that he named them after the moon and sun. This made the Norse gods very angry, and to punish him for his arrogance, they placed his children high in the heavens, forcing them to forever guide the orbs they were named for across the sky.

Because he is of mortal parentage, Mani is sometimes considered the original *man in the moon*. While there are several variations of this folktale, in most versions the man in the moon is someone who was banished from Earth for some sort of wrongdoing, so far from being a forgotten lunar god, Mani is actually a celebrated icon in nurseries all over the world!

FREYA

Another Norse deity who is strongly associated with the moon is Freya, who was one of the most important goddess of the Norse pantheon. Freya was the goddess of beauty, love, war, magic and witchcraft. It is through her link with magic and witchcraft that she is associated with the moon,

particularly the full moon, as it is the most auspicious time for spell casting. Her totem animals are cats and she is often depicted in a silver or gold chariot being drawn by a pair of wildcats. She was invoked as a goddess of fertility throughout Scandinavia. After making a deal with the god Odin, Freya could claim the souls of half the number of warriors who died in battle, and thus she is a death goddess too.

CERRIDWEN

Celtic goddess of the moon, Cerridwen is also linked to inspiration, transformation, creativity and wisdom gained through experience. She is sometimes called the Keeper of the Cauldron, for she presides over a magical cauldron that can bring the dead back to life. As a result, she is associated with the cycle of life, death and rebirth. Her totem animal is a pure-white sow, and represents fertility. She is a patron of poets, writers, artists, musicians and bards. Call on her for all issues of creativity, fertility and inspiration.

KHONSU

Khonsu, meaning *the traveller*, is the Egyptian god of the moon and time. He was said to guide and protect anyone who had to travel by night, watching over them like a guardian. For this reason, he is known as a pathfinder and a defender, similar to Saint Christopher of Christian belief. He was associated with healing and fertility. He is the master of the night and a powerful god to invoke for matters of protection, guidance and guardianship, so if you have to work the night shift he is the one to call on.

As you can see, there are lots of goddesses and gods that are linked to the moon and the lunar cycle. Although they are all lunar deities, each one has their own special attributes and totems, so do your research and read up on the deities that interest you the most.

CHAPTER FOUR

MOON SIGNS

The moon revolves around the earth and, as it does, it moves through all the signs of the zodiac, switching from one sign to the next roughly every two and a half days. Each new moon always falls within the current zodiac sign, while the full moon of that month falls into the opposing sign on the zodiac wheel. For instance, if we were currently in the zodiac sign of Scorpio, roughly 23rd October to 22nd November, then the new moon of that period would also be in Scorpio, while the full moon would be in the opposing sign of Taurus. This effectively means that the moon casts two different influences over us throughout the sign of Scorpio, so we feel a boost of Scorpio energies during the new moon and a strong influx of Taurean energy during the full moon. This same pattern is true as we pass through all the zodiac signs of the year.

Discovering your moon sign can be as complicated as you want it to be. To pinpoint the exact place the moon was in when you were born, you would need to know your time of birth and have a birth chart drawn up, but in simple terms, your moon sign influence is the one opposite the zodiac sign you were born into. So if you were born into the sun sign of Aquarius then your moon-sign influence would be Leo. Moon-sign energy can influence all of us, but it is especially powerful when either the new or full moon is in your own zodiac sign. Let's take a look at the moon signs of the zodiac and how their influences might affect you.

MOON IN ARIES

Aries is a fire sign ruled by the planet Mars, the god of war, so expect fiery tempers, short fuses and a tendency towards confrontation when this moon sign is in play. This is a great time to stand up for yourself and make your feelings known, as Aries energy surrounds you and helps you to feel strong and bold. Take care not to let this tip over into a feeling of invincibility, or you could find yourself out of your depth.

New moon – Use the bold energy of an Aries new moon to put your own needs first and take time for yourself.

Full moon – When the full moon is in Aries, keep your eyes peeled for new opportunities coming your way and be sure to make the most of them.

MOON IN TAURUS

The earth sign of Taurus is ruled by the planet Venus, the goddess of love and beauty. This moon sign influences people to take better care of themselves with self-love rituals and pampering. It can even lead you towards a new relationship, shining a light upon a new love interest or deepening the bond between long-term lovers. However, Taurus also has a no-nonsense approach to life, so practical expressions of affection are more likely during this time, rather than big romantic gestures.

New moon – This as a time for slowing down, so don't be surprised if circumstances force you into a slower pace of life for a short time. Use this time to pamper and recharge.

Full moon – Taurus energy is all about stability, so use this influence to increase your levels of overall security, be this financial or personal. Remember that building a sense of security around yourself is also a form of self-care, and take responsibility for your personal safety and home security.

MOON IN GEMINI

The air sign of Gemini is ruled by the planet Mercury, the god of communication, and this sign is certainly known for its flamboyant energies. When the moon is in Gemini, it is basically calling you out to play, filling your calendar with events and nights out. This moon sign is the party influencer, and the energies at work right now tend to make people feel adventurous and generally more playful. Take care, though, because too much Gemini energy can lower inhibitions, which leads to recklessness and taking greater risks.

New moon – Time to make plans with friends, collaborate with colleagues on a big project or set up a new website. Communication is the key, and you could find yourself going out every night or spending hours on the phone chatting.

Full moon – Use this moon to do some networking and expand your circle of friends. It's always fun to meet new people and try new things. Monitor your socializing, however, because if you burn the candle at both ends you could end up burnt out altogether.

MOON IN CANCER

The water sign of Cancer is ruled by the moon itself, giving a double whammy of lunar energies and heightening emotions during this moon sign. Emotions tend to run high under this influence, so don't be surprised if you feel hyper-sensitive or a little tearful at this time. Just as the water of the tides ebbs and flows, your emotions might be up and down for a while, leading to a sense of fragility and vulnerability. Cancerian energy is known for hiding emotions beneath a hard shell, but when the moon is in Cancer, you can expect all those hidden, repressed emotions to come to the fore.

New moon – This is a good time to retreat into your shell and spend some time in hibernation, away from the hustle and bustle of life. Go within and reflect on the emotions this moon sign has brought up for you.

Full moon – Understand that a hard shell doesn't only protect you from the hard knocks of life, it can also be a barrier from all the good things too. Use this time to learn how to be vulnerable in a safe way, perhaps with a therapist or trusted friend. Open up and explore your inner mental landscapes.

MOON IN LEO

The fire sign of Leo is ruled by the sun, making this another flamboyant sign. Unlike the party atmosphere of a Gemini moon, however, a Leo moon uses this flamboyance for furthering ambition and getting noticed for all the right reasons, both professionally and personally. This moon-sign influence will make you shine! It will draw you out into the spotlight and encourage you to be your best self. A Leo moon brings out the leadership in all of us, and you might be called upon to take charge of a situation or give a keynote speech or presentation at work. The lion likes to shake out his golden mane for all to see!

New moon – This is a good time to start fleshing out your ambitions and mapping out a path to achieve your objectives. Do you need to apply for a course or a promotion, attend interviews or auditions, or organize a networking event? Use this lunar energy to project yourself forwards into your dreams, one step at a time.

Full moon – Be bold and follow your heart. What sparks the joy in your life, what gets you fired up, what are you enthusiastic about? Use this phase to act on these spiritual prompts and follow your bliss.

MOON IN VIRGO

The earth sign of Virgo is ruled by the planet Mercury, god of communication. These lunar energies will keep you busy all month if you let them, because Virgo is the sign of hustle culture, perfectionism, organization and personal achievement. At its best, a Virgo moon will help you declutter and reorganize your entire house, but at its worst it will draw you into nit-picking perfectionism and procrastination because you cannot do something perfectly the first time around. Nothing is perfect, and while you might keep telling yourself that there is always room for improvement, eventually this kind of mentality can start to work against you, meaning that you never finish anything!

New moon – Beware of taking on too much at this time. Stick to one or two things that you know you can get done to a high standard and still have free time to decompress. Beware of becoming too critical, both of yourself and others.

Full moon – This is the time when perfectionism can go into overdrive! This is great if you need a boost of motivation, as it can drive you to achieve, but if you are already a high achiever, then watch out for hubris and a *save the world* mentality creeping in. Treat yourself to a day off!

MOON IN LIBRA

The air sign of Libra is ruled by the planet Venus, goddess of love. When this moon sign is in charge, you might be tempted to try and bring more balance to your life, perhaps by prioritizing love and family over your career, for instance. However, a classic Libran trait is that of indecision. They cannot seem to choose between two or more options, often preferring to have their cake and eat it, which can lead to fractious relationships and eventual isolation. The need to compartmentalize life is also a Libran trait, as they try to separate out aspects of their life and contain them in boxes. Eventually, though, all the contents spill out and they find themselves in a mess of their own design! Watch out for these traits when the moon is in Libra. By all means, use the energies to bring more balance into your life, but be careful not to over-compartmentalize. Accept that life is messy at times; different aspects of your world will bleed into one another, and that is as it should be. Containment will only work for so long.

New moon – Practice your decision-making skills! If you can hone this vital life skill, you will naturally bring about more balance because you will no longer be torn between several options. Plus, you'll feel more in control, as the decision will not be made for you by circumstance.

Full moon – Seek forgiveness from those who might have been hurt by your indecisiveness in the past, and set the scales of justice right. Love triangles are common when Libra energy is at play, so look to make amends for any hurt you might have caused, and heal your own emotional wounds. Emotional balance is just as important as life balance.

MOON IN SCORPIO

As a water sign, Scorpio is ruled by the planets Pluto and Mars, bringing influences of death and rebirth from Pluto, and also war and conflict from Mars. This is a heady, potent mix, meaning that when the moon is in Scorpio, tensions can run high, and intense emotions are frequently in play. These lunar energies can lead to an existential crisis. Reflecting on the deeper meaning of life, death, afterlife and the overall meaning of your own personal existence and value is common at this time. A Scorpio moon is intense, brutal, seductive, overwhelming, enticing and obsessive. It is a deep dive into humanity and what it means to be alive. It's big, powerful stuff, and it can have a profound influence on people. At best, these lunar energies teach resilience and robustness; at worst, they can lead to deep feelings of melancholia and worthlessness. This is not a moon to mess with, but one to court gently, with both passion and compassion.

New moon – This is the time to live in the moment, to live with passion! Allow life to seduce you. Be bold, be sexy and use your charms. Take hold of your power and make the most of it.

Full moon – Embrace new experiences but be aware that Scorpio has some very dark energies that can lead you into an even darker place if you are not careful. Depression, addiction, manipulation, risk-taking and so on can all come into play during this moon. Focus instead on the passion and vibrancy of Scorpio energies, let go of the past and feed your desires in a safe way.

MOON IN SAGITTARIUS

Fire sign Sagittarius is ruled by the planet Jupiter, god of thunder and the sky. When the moon is in this sign, you may feel the urge to go on an adventure, go exploring or take a trip somewhere you've never been before. A Sagittarius moon is all about taking calculated risks and trying new things. It is not about being reckless, which is more of a Scorpio moon trait. Instead, this moon suggests that something new is calling to you, something that will expand your horizons and your world view.

New moon – This is the time to change up your habits and create some new ones. Learn a new language, start a hobby or join a group or sports team. Have fun and enjoy the spirit of adventure that this lunar energy brings.

Full moon – Now is the time to break out of your comfort zone! Go travelling, volunteer for a charity, spread your wings and see what happens. The archer's energy can help you shoot for the moon, so aim as high as you can.

MOON IN CAPRICORN

The earth sign of Capricorn is ruled by the planet Saturn, bringer of dark emotions, big life lessons and melancholia. When the moon is in this sign, it can bring with it the need to excel. It influences people to press ahead, set goals, make plans and work harder, and increases their self-discipline. The moon in Capricorn is a great motivator, so if this is your moon sign, you are likely to be a very self-driven and determined character who is probably a high achiever. Not one for simply dreaming, a Capricorn moon makes you want to manifest all your wildest ambitions to the highest degree.

New moon – This is the time to decide in detail exactly what it is that you want from your life. Set your goals and start making plans to achieve them.

Full moon – Remind yourself how far you've already come! Give yourself a pat on the back and celebrate all that you have already achieved, before you look towards your long-term goals for the future. Remember to show gratitude for what you have.

MOON IN AQUARIUS

Flighty air sign Aquarius is ruled by the planets Uranus and Saturn, bringing energies of extremes and breakouts from Uranus along with Saturn's traits of life lessons and melancholia. When the moon is in Aquarius, you might act irrationally or impetuously without thinking far enough ahead to see what the consequences of your actions might be. This is the rebellious moon, the one that can make people act spontaneously, childishly and selfishly. Reality is an inconvenience; consequences are for other people to have to deal with. The lunar energies at this time can make you restless, flitting from pillar to post, bouncing off one thing straight into the next, be this in your relationships, jobs or hobbies. You might be tempted to let other people clean up your mess, or abdicate all sense of personal responsibility. An Aquarius moon carries with it a sense of unreality and a wilful ignorance of the damage done, so look before you leap!

New moon – Freedom is your watchword, so embrace your liberty and have fun! Make your wildest visions your reality – take a flying lesson, go on a speedboat or learn to ride a motorcycle. Give your rebellious spirit a safe, controlled outlet before it gets you into trouble!

Full moon – This is the time of breakthroughs, breakouts and sometimes breakdowns. You might suddenly realize that you hate your job and want to leave, or that your relationship is over. When the need to break out takes hold, make sure that you do a risk assessment and check your facts before you act on impulse. Aquarius energy is a dynamic force, so try to keep a level head.

MOON IN PISCES

Water-loving sign Pisces is ruled by the planet Neptune, god of the sea. Still waters run deep, and when the moon is in this sign you are more likely to be ruled by your emotions than by logic or common sense. A Pisces moon can be a flat calm, a tsunami or a combination of the two. Little things might trigger a storm of emotion during this time, and your empathic abilities may be heightened, meaning that you pick up on other people's emotions as well as your own, and it can be difficult to draw the line between the two. Emotional hangovers are common at this time, and you might feel more tired than usual, or have more meaningful dreams.

New moon – Use all that emotional energy by channelling it into a creative endeavour, such as painting, journalling, or composing music or poetry. Creativity can be a great balm for the emotions, offering a positive outlet so that they don't fester. Find an artistic way to get your emotions out and pin them down in a creative way.

Full moon – Strengthen your boundaries! All that empathy can have a negative impact on your wellbeing, so make sure you reinforce your personal boundaries during this moon.

CHAPTER FIVE

MOON MANIFESTATION

A ll magic is a kind of manifestation because you are attempting to bring into being something that wasn't in your reality prior to casting the spell. You can also use magic to banish something that no longer serves you, and in this sense you are manifesting a void. Witches have always manifested in tune with the moon, and we cast our spells in accordance with certain phases to bring about specific results.

The moon teaches us to have patience, even when casting for our deepest desires. It is a visual reminder that magic can take time. A general rule of thumb is that smaller spells take approximately one full lunar cycle to manifest, while bigger spells may take several months. So if you were to cast for a windfall on the new moon, you might find yourself with a pay rise by the time the next new moon comes around. Likewise, if you were casting to move house or start a family on the full moon, it could be six full moons or more before this goal manifests in your life. The bigger the goal, the longer it takes, but the moon is a constant companion as you wait for the manifestation to occur, offering you a visual cue to stay positive and keep affirming your success.

LIKE ATTRACTS LIKE

In magic, like attracts like, so what you focus on the most is what you are pulling into your life. This happens whether you are aware of it or not, and it is the reason why it pays to be positive. Negative habits and thought patterns, feelings of low self-worth, disparaging self-talk and so on can all work to bring more negative circumstances your way. Fortunately, the opposite is also true, so surrounding yourself with

positive people, habits and thought processes will bring more positive circumstances towards you. Be mindful of the energies you are sending out into the world, because that is exactly the kind of energy that will come back to you. Be optimistic, positive, gentle and kind, and that is what you will attract.

DECLARE YOUR INTENTIONS TO THE MOON

Making a declaration is a powerful thing. There is a reason that people remember the first time their partner said *'I love you'* – it's because this is a powerful declaration of an emotional bond. There is also a reason why you often say it back – because like attracts like! With this in mind, declaring your intentions to the moon can have a deep impact on your chances of success, because you are putting your goal out into the universe, confiding in the moon like an old friend.

Think of something that you want to achieve in the next month. It could be that you want to sign up to a new class, start a new hobby, make a new friend etc. Once you have your intention in mind, go outside on the night of the full moon. Look up at the bright orb in the sky and breath in her energies, then state your intention out loud or in your head. For example, you might say something like this: *'Mother moon I greet you and welcome your light, I set my intention to take up dance classes this night.'*

Now as you watch the moon move through her cycle, she will remind you each night to follow through on your intention, so that by the time she is full once more, you are already attending dance classes and living

the reality of that ambition. You can repeat this process for any goal. Just remember that bigger goals will take longer than a month to manifest.

MOON MAPPING

Another technique for manifesting with the moon is that of moon mapping. This is great for larger goals and is a good way to maintain focus and motivation. Think of a large goal that you would like to achieve, then break it down into smaller achievable tasks. Write out the phases of the moon on a sheet of paper and, alongside each phase, plot out the tasks of your goal in alignment with that moon phase. So if you wanted to start a new business, for example, your moon map might look something like this:

☽ New moon - Write a business plan.

☽ Waxing moon - Set up a website or scout for premises.

☽ Full moon - Apply for a business loan, open a business bank account and register as self-employed for tax purposes.

☽ Waning moon - Hand in your notice or reduce your hours at your current job, and clear out anything that isn't in alignment with your new business plan.

》 Dark moon - Conduct market research and product development for your business.

》 New moon - Start trading.

This type of time structuring means that you are drawing upon the energies of the moon that are in alignment with the tasks you need to perform. You can use a moon map for any goal, and you can expand the time scale so that you are mapping out several months of lunar cycles, rather than just the one, as given in the example above. The beauty of this is that the lunar cycle keeps you on track with your plans, be they long- or short-term.

EXPRESS GRATITUDE

Gratitude is a vital component of all magic and manifestation. Lack of gratitude can derail your magic in a heartbeat. Demonstrating that you appreciate what you already have will ensure that more comes to you. Traditionally, the full moon is a propitious time to offer your gratitude to the universe, but ideally you should show that you are grateful on a daily basis. Gratitude is an active pursuit, not a passive one. Here are some ideas for demonstrating gratitude:

》 Keep a gratitude journal and write down 3 to 5 things that you are grateful for each night before you go to sleep. What did the day bring that you particularly enjoyed?

☽ Light a stick of incense and allow it to burn on your moon altar as an offering of gratitude to the universe for all that you have.

☽ Donate to those in need, as this is a way of acknowledging that you are fortunate enough to have an excess. Clothes, books, baby things - whatever you have an abundance of, go through and donate some things to charity.

☽ Tithe to a charity by making a financial contribution each month to an organization you care about.

☽ Offer your time and do some volunteering. You could visit a nursing home and spend time with the elderly, or offer to babysit for a friend so she can have some downtime.

☽ Send a thank-you note to someone who has helped you in some way.

☽ Cook a meal for someone.

☽ Feed wildlife by putting out bird feeders and nuts for squirrels etc.

☽ Pick up litter to show gratitude for our beautiful planet.

☽ Show gratitude for freedom and security by assisting military veterans. Offer your time to service charities or buddy up with an ex-serviceman or woman in your area.

☽ Appreciate what you have and the people who surround you.

☽ Know that gratitude is the fastest way to experience the manifestation of your goals.

CHAPTER SIX
MOON DIVINATIONS

D ivination is the art of seeing; it's commonly known as fortune telling. It is one of the tricks of the witch's trade, and most witches practice some aspect of it. Tarot cards are perhaps the most well-known divination tool, with oracle cards coming in at a close second. If you are interested in card readings, you might find my Moon Magic card deck useful. There are lots of other ways to practice divination too. Crystals, water, mirrors and pendulums are all tools used in foretelling the future, and we will be looking at some of them in this chapter.

DARK SHADOWS

It is generally accepted that divination is a practice that should be performed after dark. Some witches refuse to do card readings and so on until the sun has set, so it is an aspect of magical living that naturally aligns with the moon. Indeed, there is something very enchanting about setting up a crystal ball or scrying vessel in the dark, with a single candle flame and the moonlight being the only illumination. In the quiet reaches of the night, the unknown becomes known through the shadows reflected in the scrying vessel used.

However, any type of divination is always subject to change, so if you do not like what the crystal ball or whatever is showing you, then you have the option to change your patterns or your approach to life in order to affect a different outcome. Nothing is set in stone, and the future is always yours to create. Divination shows only what the most likely outcome is, given the current situation. If you alter the situation, then you alter your future too. The shadows of prophecy will shift and change shape based on the decisions you make each day, so divination presents guidance only, rather than a set, unchangeable outcome.

LUNAR DIVINATION TOOLS

In this book we will concentrate on the kinds of divination tools that are linked to the moon – so crystals, mirrors and bowls of water. While some crystal balls can be expensive, you do not need to spend a lot of money, for a simple bowl of water can be used in exactly the same way as a crystal ball.

Gazing into a vessel – be it water, a mirror or crystal – in order to see images of the past, present or future is known as scrying. Your scrying vessel should always be clean and dust-free, or the water fresh and clear, to give a pure surface on which to scry. With any kind of scrying, visions can come into your mind's eye, and this is more common to begin with. With greater practice, you might start to see visions in the vessel itself. The first hint that a vision is about to appear in the vessel is when the surface suddenly seems to fill with cloud or smoke. Maintain your concentration and when the clouds clear, the vision should play out in the vessel. This does take a lot of practice, so persevere.

Crystal balls – These represent the full moon and are attuned with the Mother aspect of the Triple Goddess. The ball should be a good size without being unwieldy. Traditionally, it should fit easily into the palms of both hands, without being too heavy to hold. Ideally it should be placed on a stand, on a table laid with a black or dark-coloured cloth. This gives a shadowy background and ensures there are no gaudy patterns to interfere with the Sight.

Water – This can be a natural body of water such as a loch or lake, but it is usually a bowl of water. Scrying bowls tend to be painted black inside to give a dark surface on which to scry. Water scrying uses the exact same process and techniques as scrying in a crystal ball, but because it is a more dynamic force, you might find that visions come to you more easily. For this reason, it is common practice to begin with water scrying before moving onto crystal balls and dark mirrors.

Dark mirrors – A dark mirror, or scrying mirror, is a small mirror with a completely black surface. It could be made from a circle of black obsidian crystal, or it could be homemade, with the sliver removed from a makeup mirror and the back painted black. You can even use a TV that is turned off, as the black screen provides an instant scrying mirror! Dark scrying mirrors are probably the most difficult to master. They represent the dark moon and are attuned to the Crone. Some of them come as crystal balls too. Again, use the same techniques as with a crystal ball, but be aware that dark mirrors tend to take a bit longer to master.

TIPS FOR A SUCCESSFUL SCRYING SESSION

☽ Prepare the room by dimming the lights and lighting a single candle.

☽ Spread a black or dark-coloured cloth over a table.

☽ Place your chosen scrying vessel on the table and position yourself so that you can comfortably peer into it.

☽ Breathe slowly and evenly - don't hold your breath.

☽ Repeat a scrying chant such as the one given below.

☽ Concentrate on your question or query.

☽ Gaze into the centre of the vessel with eyes that are softly focused. Blink when necessary.

☽ Note down any visions you had during your session, which should last no longer than 30 minutes, or you will tire your eyes.

Scrying Chant

It is common practice to begin a scrying session with a special chant. This is a form of spoken intention and helps to set the tone of the session. The chant can be said out loud or whispered under your breath. You can make up your own chant or you can use this one:

Vessel deep shows visions true
Sights unseen betwixt me and you
What is unknown I now shall know
As through this vessel the visions flow
Secrets lost and truth revealed
Past, present and future now unsealed.
So mote it be

How to Make a Dark Mirror

Moon phase – Make the mirror during a dark moon.

Items required – A round picture frame about the size of a tea plate, matt-black paint and a paintbrush, or black construction paper or card.

Although you can buy a dark mirror from new-age stores or online, you can easily make your own. Take a circular picture frame to represent the moon and carefully remove the glass. Use the paint to cover the back of the glass and let it dry thoroughly. Add a second coat of paint and let this dry too. Alternatively, you could draw around the glass and cut a piece of black card to fit in the frame. Whichever method you choose, reassemble the picture frame with the black paint or card on the inside of the frame. This will keep the paint from scratching off or the card from ripping. You now have a dark mirror for your scrying sessions. Keep it on your lunar altar and use it for divination.

Lunar Stones for Divination

Moon phase – Put this divination tool together on the night of the full moon.

Items required – A small pouch, lavender oil and tumble stones of the following crystals: clear quartz, snowy quartz, red jasper, moonstone and hematite.

First sprinkle the pouch, both inside and out, with a few drops of lavender oil. This will act as a cleansing agent to keep your crystals pure and free of negative energy. Each crystal represents a phase of the lunar cycle. Place them into the pouch and give them a shake. When you want to use them, shake the pouch three times as you ask your question, then draw out a single lunar crystal. Use the guide to interpret the answer to your question.

Clear quartz – represents the new moon, meaning new beginnings are under way but as yet unseen. The shoots are about to burst through, but on the surface everything looks dead and fallow. Have faith that things

are being put into place for your highest good. You are surrounded by Maiden energy.

Snowy quartz – represents the waxing moon, meaning a time of fresh starts and planning is underway. Good things are coming to you, and you are working hard to achieve your goals. You are surrounded by positive energy.

Red jasper – represents the full moon and the blood of the Mother goddess. This is a vibrant time, and you are reaping the rewards of your labour. However, it is not without difficulty or sacrifice. The end result will be worth the pain. You are surrounded by Mother energy.

Moonstone – represents the waning moon, meaning that the hard work is done and a brief time of respite is to come. The cloudy aspect of this crystal means that you might not be able to see your way ahead right now, but trust that all will be well, given time.

Hematite – represents the dark moon, meaning that you need to rest and recharge in preparation for the next cycle of growth and activity. Something may have been stripped from your life, and you need to grieve the loss or you may be experiencing a period of fatigue. Rest, recharge and recuperate at this time. New seeds are being sown in the darkness. You are surrounded by Crone energy.

Smoke On, Go!

Moon phase – This is a good ritual for a waning or dark moon.

Items required – a cauldron or heatproof bowl, sand, charcoal blocks, a lighter; dried herbs such as mugwort, white sage, basil and mint are good ones to use.

Smoke scrying is less well known than crystal or water scrying, but it can be very relaxing and beneficial for mental health. Make sure that you are outdoors or in a well-ventilated room, away from any smoke detectors.

Fill the cauldron or bowl with sand to absorb the heat safely, then light a charcoal block and place it in the centre of the bowl. Next add the dried herbs to the charcoal block a pinch at a time, so they burn slowly. The smoke will rise quite quickly, forming patterns in the air. Watch as these patterns unfold, making special note of any images you see, such as hearts, arrows and other symbols. Use your intuition to interpret what these images mean for you. If the smoke is bringing the image towards you, that is a sign that it is coming your way, but if the smoke carries it away from you, then it is not meant to be, or will not happen for a long while. If the image travels straight up, the timing is as yet unclear. If the charcoal block goes out or the herbs don't burn, then it is not meant to be.

You can enhance your smoke-scrying sessions by backlighting the smoke with a coloured light, such as a pink salt lamp. This gives the smoke added definition and makes it easier to scry out images and patterns.

Mother of Dark and Light

Moon phase – Make this stone at the time of the full moon.

Items required – a round pebble or stone, black paint, white paint and two paintbrushes, clear varnish.

As you have seen throughout this book, the moon and the Mother goddess she represents is both light and dark, waxing and waning, Mother and Crone. We can tap into both these energies in divination.

Divination need not be complicated, and sometimes all you need is a simple yes or no answer to a simple question. This is known as *binary divination*. The most popular binary-divination tool is the pendulum, but you can also make a simple *binary stone* to achieve the same results. First find a pebble on the beach or the riverside. It should be roundish to represent the moon, and it should feel nice in your hand. Take it home with you and paint one side white to represent the answer *Yes*. Allow the paint to dry, then turn the stone over and paint the other side black to represent the answer *No*. Wait for the paint to dry before varnishing the entire stone to protect the paint. To use the stone, ask a simple binary question, then toss the stone in the air like you would a coin and see which side faces up when it lands. If the white side is facing upwards the answer to your question is yes, while if the black side is facing up the answer is no.

CHAPTER SEVEN

SHADOW CRAFT

Moon magic isn't only about spell craft and astrological signs and symbols. It is also about the shadow craft in the darker reaches of the mind, the conscious and the unconscious, and how they work together to create your reality. The light of the moon is mesmeric and meditative, sometimes full and bright, sometimes hidden by cloud, but always powerful. In the same way, the unconscious mind is always working away, although we are frequently unaware of it. Programming the unconscious mind is a way of ensuring that your inner landscape remains positive and doesn't sabotage your chances of success. Likewise, you can tap into your unconscious mind, also known as the higher self, for guidance and self-support.

FINDING QUIET AMID CHAOS

The world can seem like quite a chaotic place at times, and it can be difficult to keep that chaos from impacting your life and your mental wellbeing. However, being able to find a sense of calm and quiet amid this chaos is essential if you are to maintain peace of mind. Chaos, panic, fear and anxiety are all infectious, so it is vital that you learn to create your own boundary of mental peace and quiet. Think of the poem *If* by Rudyard Kipling and learn to *'keep your head when all about are losing theirs and blaming it on you'*!

Recognizing the first stirrings of chaos is often half the battle. If you know that your workplace is stretched to breaking point at certain times, or you know that certain people carry drama with them like a torch of doom, then you can prepare yourself for the madness in advance.

Sometimes, though, chaos comes out of the blue. Accidents, illnesses and bereavements can all take us by surprise, bringing a certain amount of chaos with them, which is unavoidable. Try using this magical technique to find a space of calm and quiet when your environment turns frenzied.

MOONLIGHT SHIELD VISUALIZATION

Go to a quiet place and close your eyes. Breathe deeply three or four times. This will help to calm your nerves. Now, in your mind's eye, visualize the full moon high in the sky, shining her light down on you. Feel the silvery rays on your skin and bathe in this imaginary light. In this way you are tapping into the lunar energies, even if it's midday, through the power of visualization. Next, imagine that the lunar rays form a shield of light all around you, sealing you in and keeping any negative chaos or drama at bay. Within this shield you are calm and peaceful, capable and strong. Once you can see yourself surrounded by a magical shield of moonlight, open your eyes, take three more deep breaths and go back out into the fray, knowing that you can handle the chaos by presenting the light of peace and calm.

SCHEDULE PSYCHIC QUIET TIME

Lunar energies are quiet by nature. While the sun can be brash and obnoxious, the moon is gentle and subtle. The nighttime energies are ones we often ignore, preferring the company of the family sitting around the TV on a dark night to that of the stars and moon – but communing with the night is a great way to enhance your psychic abilities and instincts.

There is something magical about being awake when most people are fast asleep, and the wee small hours of the night hold enchantment within them. The dark night holds onto the magical hours of storytelling – the witching hour of midnight, the devil's hour of 3am and the fairy hours of dusk and dawn. Try to schedule some psychic quiet time around these hours, perhaps going for a walk at dusk or dawn, or conducting a midnight scrying session or card reading. Perhaps you could do some stargazing during the devil's hour, in the safety of your garden (or a friend's). Provided you are sensible and do not put yourself at risk, there is no reason why you cannot enjoy the nocturnal hours to your witchy heart's content. Enjoy the magic of the nightscape and commune with the moon.

MEDITATION

Meditation is another great way to attune with the inner reaches of the mind and that which is hidden. Just like the moon, your higher self is always there, but you may not always listen to its wisdom, so meditating gives your higher self a chance to communicate with your conscious mind. In meditation you are inviting your subconscious to take centre stage for a time, to offer advice, encouragement and guidance.

Meditation has many benefits, both mentally and physically. Spending time in it can help you relax; it reduces levels of stress and anxiety, and can alleviate feelings or irritability or restlessness. It is also good for increasing your sense of self-awareness and emotional intelligence. It also develops your patience and sense of control over your emotions.

Building a meditative exercise into your magical practice is a fantastic way to learn about visions, pre-cognition and prophecy, dream worlds and other realms, the meaning of signs and symbols etc. In addition, it helps to develop your visualization skills, and in turn your ability to envision and manifest a better future for yourself, so there are really no reasons not to give it a try! Guided meditations such as the one below are often the best to begin with because, as the name suggests, they take you on a mental journey, guiding you through an imaginary realm before bringing you back to the current moment in time. A guided mediation, also known as a path-working, is a bit like mindfulness but with story-telling attached! Try the path-working below and see what it brings up for you.

Persephone's Labyrinth of the Dark Moth

For this guided meditation, it is useful to have someone read it out loud to you, or alternatively you can record it in advance so that you can play it back whenever you want to. Lie down in a comfortable position and close your eyes. Breathe deeply for a while, until you start to feel nicely relaxed, then proceed to visualize the guided meditation below.

You find yourself standing on a forest path. The night air is bracing and chill. The moon above is bright and full, lighting your way. You set off walking through the woods. In the distance you hear a soft voice whispering your name. It sounds as if the dry autumn leaves are calling out to you. You follow the path through the woods until you come to a moss-covered cave.

A lady stands at the mouth of the cave, wearing a flowing gown in the dark colours of autumn: mulberry,

grey, bronze and deep purple. A lacy network of cobwebs
is draped over the fabric, bejewelled with dewdrops
which glimmer in the moonlight, and a sweeping train
falls from the gown, made up of dry autumn leaves. Her
hair falls in a dark curtain, almost to her knees, and
her dark eyes have a glint of amber gold within them.
She is Persephone, Lady of the Underworld, Mistress of
Shadows and Spirits. She beckons you to follow her and
you walk behind her down a steep path, tangled with
tree roots and overhung with boughs of fir trees, until
you find yourself in a grove of trees and the beginning of
a labyrinth.

'Welcome to my dark labyrinth, Shadow Weaver.
Shall we venture into its centre to see who awaits?' You
nod your head and follow Persephone as she leads you
along the winding path of the labyrinth. As she walks, she
begins to chant, and you join in with her song.

'Ever circling, ever turning, take me to the centre;

Ever constant, ever changing, moving to the centre.'

After a time, you find yourself in the very centre of
the labyrinth, where a stone pillar supports a beautiful

ornate lantern. Persephone moves to the lantern, lights the candle within and says:

'At the centre of all things is the light of all lights, the light of Spirit and the light of hope, reflecting the promise of the moon above.'

The ornate knot-work of the lantern casts dancing shadows around the labyrinth. The fir trees sway in the breeze, seeming to dance in the candlelight. A tiny black moth flies out of the darkness to the light of the lantern. Again and again the little moth flies against the lantern and you watch in fascination until, in a single quick movement, Persephone reaches out and gently catches the moth. It sits peacefully in her hand and you take a closer look at its beautiful, dark markings.

'Light any spark in the dark and the moth will come, for he is eternally drawn to the deeper darkness beyond the flame. As he struggles to reach the shadow-side of candlelight, he exerts himself, constantly striving to reach his dark goal, until he is his own undoing. For of course it is an illusion, and the moth will never attain the deeper darkness, except in his own demise.

'Human nature is very similar. You have a tendency to believe that circumstances are somewhat blacker and darker than they really are, so you do not see the light. You forget to respect its heat and warmth, so you become burned by sorrow. Remember that in the darkest of times, the light is always there, if you only look for it.' Persephone blows gently on the moth and it flies away into the night, unscathed by its brush with fire.

'Go now, Shadow Weaver, and walk the labyrinth back to your own realm.' You leave Persephone in the middle of the labyrinth and take the circling path back out into the woods. Eventually you see the cave and the path back to the world of consciousness.

When you feel ready, open your eyes and become aware of your surroundings. Write down your mediation experiences, and how Persephone's words have resonated with you, in your moon journal, then go about your day.

MOON JOURNAL

If you haven't started a moon journal yet, then I urge you to do so. Traditionally, magical journals are handwritten, but you can start a digital one if you prefer, or add a moon magic section to your current Book of Shadows if you have one. Use the moon journal to keep track of your meditations, spells, rituals, manifestations and so on. It is also wise to make a note of how the moon affects your moods and behaviours as she moves through her cycle. Do you feel most powerful at the full moon during the time of the Mother, or during a waning or dark moon during the time of the Crone? How does a new moon make you feel: optimistic, nervous or restless? Keeping a moon journal will reinforce your connection to lunar energies, and you can record your most successful rituals so you can repeat the patterns that work for you. Remember that all magic is a personal journey, and your path is a unique one that only you are destined to tread. Here are some tips for what to add to your moon journal:

☽ Favourite crystals and the lunar energies they work best with;

☽ The moon cycle and how it reflects in your moods;

☽ Herbs and night-flowering blooms you can use in lunar spells;

☽ Your dreams and how they alter throughout the moon's phases;

☽ Your patterns of concentration – does the moon have an impact?

☽ Favourite spells and rituals for attuning with the moon;

☽ Lunar deities and their attributes;

☽ Lunar totems you would like to work with in rituals;

☽ Different moon names from different cultures – or devise your own;

☽ Esbat rituals and traditions.

CHAPTER EIGHT

DARK NIGHTS OF DREAMING

Your dreams are far more than somnambulistic rambles through nighttime realms of wonder and imagination. They are a way to process life events, work through your emotions, face fears and even find solutions to problems. Everyone dreams. It is a natural part of your nightly sleeping pattern. However, you may not always remember your dreams. Sometimes they fade almost as soon as you have opened your eyes, while at other times the dream is so vivid it stays with you for the rest of the day.

Many people believe that the moon has a profound effect on their dreams and their sleeping patterns in general. It is not uncommon to have a more restless night and more vivid dreams during a full moon, for instance. This could be because the night sky is much brighter, making a deep, dreamless sleep more difficult.

You might also see the moon in your dreams, with different lunar phases thought to signify different things. Dreaming of a new moon could mean that a fresh challenge is on the way, while a full moon denotes success. Dreaming of a waning or dark moon, or the moon hidden by mist or cloud, is thought to represent something that is hidden or repressed, weighing on your mind. Dreaming is a magical experience in its own right. In your dreams you can fly, have superpowers, win the lotto or meet your idols. There are no limits. A whole world of possibility is open to you as you slumber. You will spend approximately one third of your life asleep, so with all this going on, it makes sense to try and harness such power, or at the very least understand it a little better.

AND SO TO BED...

Creating a peaceful nighttime routine is the first step in harnessing your nocturnal visions. You need to feel safe, warm and comfortable in order to have a good night's sleep. You should also be as relaxed as possible, and for this purpose lavender is your best friend. Begin your night routine with a lavender-scented bath or shower. There are hundreds of lavender-based bath and body products on the market for all budgets, so you should be able to find something you like. Next, open the bedroom window slightly to allow the night air to circulate, and draw the blinds if you wish – or leave them open to the moon's rays.

Ensure that your bed is as comfy as you can make it, without it being stifling. The idea is to cocoon yourself in soft nightwear and bedclothes. Scent your bedding with a lavender pillow spray or a few drops of lavender oil. You could also burn a lavender-scented candle for half an hour before you turn out the light and go to sleep. Grab a relaxing drink such as hot chocolate or a special cup of nighttime tea, and curl up under the duvet with a good book. Sip your tea and read until you feel drowsy, then blow out the candles, turn off the lights and sleep, perchance to dream.

THE PSYCHOLOGY OF SLEEPING POSITIONS

Your preferred sleeping position says a lot about your state of mind, and psychologists have come up with interesting interpretations for each posture. While we move through many positions each night, the one that you habitually adopt is your natural preference.

Fetal – curled up, with knees brought up to the chest and arms tucked in. This is the position of the babe in the womb, and the most common sleeping position. Both children and adults adopt this pose. It indicates a fairly relaxed person, though it can also relate to shyness and timidity. Interestingly, it is often the position adopted by someone who is going through a trauma of some kind, reflecting their inner feelings of insecurity and the need to curl up and protect themselves. People often adopt this position when they need to have a good cry.

Log – sleeping on the side, legs and arms straight down. This denotes a fairly balanced individual, one who is open to others and quite sociable. However, there is also a total lack of defence in this position, which means that it can be easy to take advantage of this person.

Yearning – another side position, but this time the sleeper might have one leg slightly bent, as if stepping forward. Also the arms tend to be reaching out away from the body, as if trying to hold onto something. This is perhaps the most vulnerable of the poses, indicating a fragile personality who has in all likelihood experienced trauma of some kind. The outstretched arms could just as easily be used for defence, though, and this denotes a lack of trust in others and a willingness to stand up for themselves.

Soldier – flat on the back, legs slightly apart, arms relaxed by the side. This is the pose of complete confidence! This *sunbathing* position indicates someone with a strong sense of self, one who is comfortable being the centre of attention. They know who they are and what they want from life, and they are ready to go out and get it. However, the soldier is always on high alert, and this individual might have trouble truly relaxing and letting go of control.

Freefall – flat on the stomach, face turned to one side, arms bent at the elbows with the hands raised. This is the position of someone who is completely closed off from others. It is a pose of self-protection, as all the vital organs are tucked in close to the mattress and the heart is turned away, as the sleeper presents their back to the room. This denotes someone who is suspicious and who does not trust or open up to other people very easily.

Starfish – flat on the back, arms and legs spread wide, reaching towards the four corners of the mattress and taking up as much room as possible. This denotes someone who is always ready to help other people. They are ready to leap into action at a moment's notice and enjoy being of service to others, yet it can lead to a martyr mindset or overextending oneself if not carefully monitored.

TYPES OF DREAMS

There are various types of dreams, from those that recur over and over again to the terror of the nightmare. Most of us experience a wide variety of dreams, often experiencing two or three types within the same night.

Keeping a record can help you to identify the kind of dreams you have and how the moon might be affecting them. Lots of people like to write down their dreams as soon as they wake up, keeping a note pad and pen by the bed for this purpose. You could also make a voice note on your phone.

Whatever way you choose to record your dreams, it is highly likely that they will fall into one of the following categories:

Precognitive dreams – Usually these are visions of something that has yet to happen, and are also known as annunciation dreams. You might dream that you have a baby, then discover that you are pregnant, or you might dream that you get your ideal job etc.

Lucid dreams – This is when you have the sudden realization, within the dream, that you are in fact dreaming and it is not real. Often, people wake up shortly after becoming lucid in their dreams; but if you can manage to remain asleep, sometimes you can take control of the dream and direct it like a movie. This takes practice, though.

Incubated dreams – This is when you have asked for a very specific dream to come to you, perhaps for guidance or answers to a problem.

Recurring dreams – dreaming of the same thing over and over again. Pay special attention to these dreams, as they are usually a message from your higher self. Once you act upon the message, the dreams will stop.

Visitation dreams – dreaming of the dead. These dreams often happen on special anniversaries such as birthdays or the anniversary of the death. They bring comfort and guidance and should not be discounted as imagination. Waking up can be tough, though, as the loss is felt once more.

Nightmares – Also known as night terrors, these dreams urge us to face our fears. Common nightmares, which we all have, include being chased or hunted, falling from a great height, being naked in public, being laughed at on stage, crashing a car or plane, drowning, and failing some kind of exam or test.

DREAMING OF A PAST LIFE

In addition to the types of dreams above, you might also experience dreams that show a life you lived before, in a different incarnation. In these past-life dreams you are likely to have a completely different appearance, which becomes apparent only when you do something mundane in the dream, such as look in a mirror or brush out your hair. Such dreams might be accompanied by a feeling of déjà vu or a sense of knowing that you are seeing visions of the past. People might call you by a different name, or you will be surrounded by faces you don't know but feel connected to. Often you and those around you will be wearing clothes from a different time period. It is also not unusual in these dreams to see how you died. It might feel brutal at the time, but check your birthmarks when you wake up, as these are said to be leftover traumatic injuries from past lives. Do you have a birthmark that matches an injury or death blow from a past-life dream? If so, it could be your soul's way of reminding you that you have many lifetimes of experience and wisdom to draw upon.

DREAMWEAVER

Dream incubation is the practice of requesting that a particular type of dream come to you within the next few nights. There are many reasons why you might decide to do this. It could be that you wish to connect with your ancestors or a deceased loved one via a visitation dream, or you want to experience a past-life dream or a lucid dream that you can control. Whatever your reasons, sleeping on an issue can be hugely beneficial, so try this ritual and see what turns up in the night, as you allow your dreams to tell you a bedtime story.

How to Incubate a Dream

To begin, think about the kind of dream you want to have and write it down on a piece of paper. You might put something like *I wish to meet my deceased grandmother in dreams because I miss talking to her*. Once you have the intention of the dream written down, add a drop of lavender essential oil to the paper, then fold it and place it inside your pillow case. Sprinkle a drop or two of the oil onto the pillow case, lie down and relax. Whisper what you want to dream about into your pillow as you fall asleep. This might not work immediately, but within the next seven nights, the dream you requested should manifest itself. Just be sure to write it down when you wake up!

A Pouch for Sweet Dreams

Magic can be time-consuming, but at some point amid all your moon rituals you will need to sleep. You can't stay up casting spells all night, every night! So here is a little charm bag to ensure that you enjoy sweet dreams when you go to bed. Take a small pouch and place inside it the following crystals: moonstone for dreaming, amethyst for protection, rose quartz for love and obsidian to represent nighttime. Next add the following dried herbs: lavender for deep sleep, camomile for calm and mugwort for prophetic visions. Give the pouch a good shake to mix up the contents and place it in the light of the moon for one full lunar month, new moon to new moon. Then place it under your mattress or hang it from a bedpost to work its magic and fill your nocturnal mind with the sweetest dreams. Remember that bedtime can be a magical experience as well as a relaxing one. Sweet dreams!

CHAPTER NINE
LUNAR TOTEM ANIMALS

Some creatures have long been linked with the moon. Cats, wolves, owls, hares and so on are all thought to have a special connection with the lunar cycle. In magic, witches often call upon the attributes of particular animals for certain spells or needs. So you might call upon the spirit of the cat for greater autonomy, for instance, or the wolf for team building. This is known as invoking the spirit of the animal, and it is easily done.

INVOKING YOUR TOTEM ANIMAL

You can light candles if you wish, but they are not necessary. Invoking a power animal can be as simple as closing your eyes and asking that animal spirit to guide and protect you. Alternatively, you could wear a charm or bring images and ornaments that represent your chosen power animal into your home. Here are a few of the most well-known lunar totem animals.

Wolves

The image of a lone wolf howling at the moon is an iconic one. Howling is how wolves communicate, after all, and like most hunter animals, they like to take advantage of the bright night on a full moon. They also howl to find a mate, making their presence known by scenting an area and then howling to draw attention to themselves.

Wolves have no natural predators, which means that technically they are at the top of the food chain – humans require guns and traps to defeat them, and so we have usurped their place. Wolves are now a protected species in some parts of the world, and although, sadly, they are extinct in Britain, their numbers are gradually increasing in parts of Europe. They have been unfairly demonized in popular culture, as have witches, so it should come as no surprise that many witches like to work with the spirit of the wolf as a totem creature. They are resilient, brave, loyal and great survivalists. The old saying *the wolf is at the door* refers to a time of hardship and poverty, indicating that one needs to be strategic in survival, just as a wolf would be. As a power animal, you can call on the wolf for all issues of courage, courting, family, team building, hunting out a good deal or creative survival strategies to get you through lean times.

Cats

If you have ever tried to keep a cat indoors on the night of the full moon, you will know how difficult it is! These little hunters love the moonlight and enjoy their nighttime revels. Even house cats tend to act differently during a full moon, often being more playful as they 'hunt' their toys. The cat is probably the best-known witch's familiar, too, and they do tend to take an interest in magic. They might flip your tarot cards, grab at your pendulum or stare into the flame of a fire or candle.

We can learn a lot from cats. They are such autonomous creatures, often spending their time with neighbours so that no-one ever truly 'owns' them. They seem fearless, traversing the neighbourhood at night without a care in the world. They do what they want, when they want, and they don't care what anyone else thinks of them. Cats have great confidence, and they are not afraid to defend themselves when they have to. As a power animal, the spirit of the cat can help you to become more confident, independent, fearless and free-thinking.

Stags and deer

As creatures of Artemis, stags and deer are inextricably linked with the moon and the hunt. They are prey animals, so they tend to be very highly strung and easily spooked by loud noises and the unexpected. Although their instinct is to herd together, in the autumn the stag rut takes place, so you may come across a lone stag at this time of year, as he is looking for rival stags to fight. They are formidable opponents, yet they can be surprisingly gentle with people, so long as you are quiet and respectful if you are fortunate enough to interact with them. While they will never be tame, the stags especially seem to like a certain amount of human contact, coming quite close out of curiosity, though the doe deer are much more shy.

The white hart is a pure-white stag that is said to hold magical powers. It is a popular icon of Medieval art and literature, and a symbol of the hunt. In some depictions, the white hart holds the full moon between his antlers, and as the monarch of the glen, he is said to be a royal beast. Magically speaking, he is of course an aspect of the Horned God of witchcraft. As a power animal, he can be invoked for issues of self-worth, pride, protection, abundance and prosperity.

Owls

The owl is a bird of two halves. In some cultures, it is said to represent wisdom, magic and alchemical knowledge, while in others it is thought to

be a bird of ill omen that brings bad luck. In most places, it is considered unlucky to see an owl flying during the day. In this respect the owl has a reputation for bringing melancholy on all who see it flying in daylight. As a nocturnal creature, the owl is intrinsically linked to the moon, with its round face being reminiscent of the full moon. Some people believe that the owl is an omen of death, and there is some truth to this, for it is likely that this association came about because the barn owl in particular will let out a piercing shriek of victory when it has caught its prey. In Scotland the owl is the bird of the Cailleach, the goddess of winter, and it is said that she can shape-shift into one of these birds to go around unnoticed. In most cultures, owls are associated with goddesses and the divine feminine.

Magically, owls are linked to the underworld and the dark half of the year, which is when they are at their most vocal. They are said to be great protectors of magical people, with shamans and druids of the past often wearing an owl feather to denote their standing as a holy man. It is a bird that represents the darker aspects of life: death, winter, nighttime, secret knowledge, hidden ways, balance and polarity. As a power animal, the owl can be invoked for issues of academic learning, life lessons, dark nights of the soul, shadow craft, inner wisdom, self-awareness, illness, grief and acceptance of a loss.

Frogs and toads

Frogs and toads are sometimes thought of as ugly creatures, and there is a lot of folklore and superstition to suggest that they may have been severely punished for not being attractive enough! In the past it was common to boil a live toad, or impale it on a branch, after rubbing it onto warts. This was thought to remove the wart. Some frogs and toads are toxic, so they were 'harvested' for their poison too. Frogs tended to fare better than toads, as they were thought to bring good luck, while toads were associated with bad luck. Again, this superstition could simply be down to the fact that frogs have a greater level of *pretty privilege*, which afforded them some protection!

As creatures of twilight, frogs and toads are most vocal at the rising and setting of the moon, during the hours of dawn and dusk. They are said to be a sign of rain, good harvest and female fertility, which is why kissing a frog was thought to bring a lover; but bear in mind that some frogs carry toxins in their skin, so take care if you decide to try this! In some Eastern cultures, frogs represent prosperity. In the past they were said to be witches' familiars and witches in disguise. As power animals, frogs and toads can be called upon for issues of transformation, fertility, weather witching, inner beauty, self-acceptance and abundance.

Hares

Like the wolves who howl at the moon and the cats who hunt in its light, the hare is often mesmerized by lunar light, sitting still and looking up in captivation. To see a moon-gazing hare is said to be extremely fortunate and brings good luck. The hare is a creature of the divine feminine, and is linked with fertility, spring and regeneration. In Medieval times, people believed that the image of a hare could be seen on the moon, similarly to the man in the moon.

Traditionally, a hare is thought to be an omen of thunderstorms, and in Britain it is the spirit of the corn, often seen loping through the stubble after the harvest. Long considered to be witches' familiars, it was said that an accused witch would shape-shift into a hare in order to escape her accusers, bounding away before they had a chance to catch her and put her to the rope or the fire. White hares were said to be the spirits of young women who were jilted or betrayed by their lovers. The white-hare spirit would haunt the faithless lover in his dreams until he went mad. White hares are also linked with the season of winter, ghosts and death. As a power animal, the hare can be called upon for issues of fertility, renewal, magic, divination, escaping a tormentor and going underground or retreating for some quiet time alone.

These are just a few of the animals that are associated with the moon. There are many more, so feel free to do your own research. Working with power animals can be an extremely rewarding practice, as you begin to learn more about your chosen creature and its unique strategies for survival. It is a valuable aspect of traditional magical practice, and as your totem communicates with you through dreams and visions, don't be surprised if your dreams become more vivid after calling on your totem in this way.

CHAPTER TEN
MOON RITUALS

Beautiful and mesmeric, powerful and magnetic, the moon deserves to be celebrated in ritual. In witchcraft, we call rituals that honour the moon Esbats. Each month, witches will work rituals to welcome and honour certain lunar phases, predominantly the new and full moon. We also like to make the most of special moons, such as Blue Moons and Super Moons. Dark moon is considered a time of rest, but even this is a way to honour her because the dark moon represents the fallow period before a new season of growth. In resting during the dark moon, witches are honouring that phase by their lack of action. In this chapter, we will look at some of the most common forms of Esbat ritual.

Drawing Down the Moon

D rawing down the moon is a full-moon Esbat, and it is a key aspect of Wiccan practice. It is a form of spiritual channelling, wherein the practitioner invokes the lunar goddess energies into themselves for greater power. This power is then redirected into spell craft. This Esbat is about welcoming the power of the full moon into yourself and your life. It could be described as a more active form of moon bathing, where you take the moon's energy into yourself, rather than just basking in her silvery rays. When done correctly, a sense of deep calm is experienced, along with a strong pull toward your destiny. This is why people sometimes change their mind about the type of spell they're going to cast after drawing down the moon, because the lunar energies are guiding them towards a higher path. If this happens to you, just go with it and trust that you are being guided to cast the kind of spell that is for your highest good, one that will have the best outcome for you in the long term.

To draw down the moon, you will need to have a clear view of the full moon, so you should ideally work this ritual outdoors. Traditionally you would use an athame – a witch's ritual blade – but you can also use your hand. Stand and gaze at the moon until you feel relaxed and centred. Then hold your arms out to the moon, pointing your athame or holding your hands out towards it as if you were going to capture the light. Visualize the moon's energies surging down the blade or through your hands into your body. Make a mental note of any particular feelings you experience, such as a tingling excitement or a calm sense of purpose. Once you feel that you are full of lunar energies, give thanks and lower your arms. Welcome the full moon with the following words:

'I welcome the goddess of full lunar light
I cast in your name this sacred night'

You are now ready to cast your chosen spells, using the lunar energies within you as a power boost to your magic. Traditionally, women would draw down the moon while men would draw down the sun during a midday ritual. However, in recent years it has become more common for either sex to draw down the energies of either the moon or the sun.

New Moon Esbat Ritual

Ｎew moon Esbats tend to be all about intentionality. At this time, you should decide what it is that you want the lunar energies to bring your way through the course of the coming month. Asking the moon to guide you to your goals is a great way to begin any spell work for goals, ambitions and manifestation.

On the night of the new moon, write down your intentions for the month and what you hope to accomplish. Once you have your goals written down, roll the paper into a scroll, light the end and allow it to burn in a heatproof dish or cauldron, as you say:

'New moon of lunar light
Bring me a month of success so bright'

Scatter the ashes to the sky and know that you have set your intentions and you have the magic of the moon on your side.

Blue Moon Esbat

The Blue Moon is the magical moon of manifestation! When there are two full moons in any one calendar month, the second is called the Blue Moon. It usually only occurs every couple of years – hence the saying *once in a Blue Moon*. Because it is rare, it is considered a most auspicious time for goal-setting, spell-casting and general manifestation. To tap into the sacred power of this moon, witches usually cast spells for big ambitions and long-term goals. This is the time to cast for a new house, a change in location, a marriage, a career change and so on. Basically, if it feels too big for you to achieve on your own and you have no idea how you can bring your dream into reality, then you need to harness the power of a Blue Moon.

For this ritual, you will need an egg and a marker pen. On the night of the Blue Moon, write your big ambition on the shell of the egg. Reduce the ambition down to one or two key words or a brief sentence if possible, so you might write, *I work from home,* or *I am a mother.* Be sure to write your goal in the present tense, as if it has already happened. Next, take the egg outside into the garden or an earthy space, dig a small hole and bury the egg in the earth, saying:

'As the Blue Moon shines in space and time
It lights the way to this dream of mine'

As the egg decomposes, it will slowly release the magic that you have cast and the power of the Blue Moon will begin to shift things around in your favour. This is a great ritual to cast when you know exactly where you want to be in life, but you don't know how to get there. Allow the Blue Moon energies to smooth out the path for you, so that your goal manifests naturally.

Black Moon Esbat

The Black Moon occurs when two new moons fall within the same calendar month, and again this is indicative of a time of rare moments. When the Black Moon shines, you are being given another shot at something that means a lot to you – a second bite of the cherry, so to speak. The Black Moon is the time of second chances, double takes, lucky breaks and the return of an opportunity your thought was lost to you. Keep your eyes peeled for signs that second chances are being offered, and help them along with this ritual. Take a pinch of blessing seeds, also known as nigella seeds, outside under the light of the Black Moon. Think of something in your life that you feel you missed out on, something you regret losing. It could be an old flame, a lost career opportunity or an event. Whatever it is, hold this image in your mind as you look up to the sky and the first sliver of moonlight. Now blow the seeds in the direction of the moon and say:

'As a Black Moon edges into view
A second chance returns anew'

Learn from your past mistakes. If fear held you back before, accept the second chance with courage. If you let other things hold you back, step forward into this new opportunity with confidence. Take that second bite of the cherry and enjoy it!

Super Moon Esbat

T he Super Moon is linked to achievement and success, so this Esbat is all about manifesting the rewards of your endeavours. However, you will be expected to work hard for your achievements; nothing is going to be handed to you on a plate. This success could come in any area of your life: love, career, business, family, adventure etc. But when you welcome the energies of the Super Moon into your life, know that you are about to experience the kind of power surge that only comes from victory. While feeling victorious is a good thing, it can also make people complacent and arrogant. Take care not to let this level of success go to your head, and keep your ego in check. To welcome the Super Moon, burn three dried bay leaves on a charcoal block and say:

'I welcome the surge of a Super Moon
Hear my request and grant this boon'
(state your goal)

Bay leaves are symbolic of victory, so burning them in an offering will ensure that you are victorious in your endeavours and ambitions. This powerful moon can guide you towards your destiny, so pay attention to the dreams you have during this moon, as they may hold key messages from the divine feminine.

PLANETARY INFLUENCES

Alongside the moon, the planets can also have an influence on you and how you view the world. Each planet represents a different aspect of character and you can draw on certain planetary energies to give you a boost in that area. For instance, if you were looking for love, you would work with Venus, lighting candles and incense as offers to this planetary goddess and invoking her in your rituals. Here are the main planets and how they can be used to build up your character, helping you become a well-rounded individual who isn't easily fazed by life's little stumbles.

Sun – rules your self-image and confidence

Moon – rules your emotional intelligence

Mercury – rules your intellect and how you communicate with others

Venus – rules your ability to give and receive love and open up to others

Mars – rules your world view and assertiveness

Jupiter – rules your destiny and luck

Saturn – rules your self-discipline and sense of personal responsibility

Uranus – rules your individuality and self-expression

Neptune – rules your imagination and dreams

Pluto – rules your self-actualization, motivation and ambition

LITTLE STAR

Wishing on stars is something lots of people have done without even being aware that they are casting a spell! It is something that we teach children to do from a very young age, and many cultures throughout history, including the Greeks and Egyptians, believed in its power. So what have you got to lose? Here are some ways that you can start wishing on stars.

)) Wish on the first star you see each night. This is usually the planet Venus, who shines brightest at dusk and dawn. Gaze at her beauty and make that wish.

)) Wish on the constellation of your astrological sign. These are the stars that you were born under, so you are naturally attuned to their energies.

)) Wish on a shooting star. These are actually meteor showers that shoot across the night sky. Meteor-shower calendars are available online, so you can look up when the next one is due, to give yourself the best chance of seeing these stunning 'shooting stars'.

Conclusion

Shoot for the Moon!

From astrology to Wicca, to shooting stars and magical planets, I hope that this little book has served to whet your appetite for making magic with the heavenly bodies. Moon magic and ritual is a fascinating topic, and now that you have read this introduction to it, you might want to delve deeper and read more about it, so take a look at the Further Reading section for some book recommendations.

Remember that we are all made of the same atoms as make up the universe, so we are all made from stardust. The planets might be a long way away, but we are certainly connected to them both spiritually and naturally by their influence on the earth and their place within our solar system.

Understanding the moon can help you to understand yourself a little better, from your moods to your dreams, so I hope that you will take some time to try out some of the rituals and techniques in the pages of this book. Use the lunar energies to propel your life forward and allow her silvery beams to carry you through adversity to the stars. The power is always there, so tap into it. Wish on stars, align with the planets and above all, always shoot for the moon! *Per ardua ad astra*.

Farewell until our next merry meeting…
Blessed Be,
Marie Bruce X

Further Reading

BOOKS BY THE SAME AUTHOR
Wicca
Celtic Spells
Moon Magic book and card deck
Book of Spells
Green Witchcraft
Wicca for Self-Transformation

BOOKS ABOUT THE MOON
DRIESEN, Tamara (2020). *Luna,* UK, Penguin Random House

GALENORN, Yasmine (2000). *Embracing the Moon*, USA, Llewellyn Publications

GALLAGHER, Kirsty (2020). *Lunar Living,* UK, Yellow Kite Books

GREENLEAF, Cerridwen (2017). *Moon Spell Magic,* USA, Mango Publishing

KANE, Aurora *(2020). Moon Magic,* USA, Quarto Publishing Group

McCOY, Edain (1998). *Lady of the Night,* USA, Llewellyn Publications

MOOREY, Teresa (2003). *Silver Moon,* UK, Ebury Press, Random House

Acknowledgements

I am grateful to my mother for her suggestion that I include some Native American folklore in this book and for her constant support of my dreams.

Thanks Mum, love you to the moon and back xxx